MW01259619

MOVIE TRIOS FOLIO

Playable on ANY THREE INSTRUMENTS
or any number of instruments in ensemble

Arranged by Michael Story

Alfred

ISBN-10: 0-7390-6325-1
ISBN-13: 978-0-7390-6325-5

BELIEVE
(From "The Polar Express" - 2004)

Words and Music by
ALAN SILVESTRI and GLEN BALLARD
Arranged by MICHAEL STORY

PERCUSSION

AS TIME GOES BY
(From "Casablanca" - 1942)

Words and Music by
HERMAN HUPFELD
Arranged by MICHAEL STORY

33536

4

CAN'T FIGHT THE MOONLIGHT
(From "Coyote Ugly" - 2000)

Words and Music by
DIANE WARREN
Arranged by MICHAEL STORY

Moderate rock

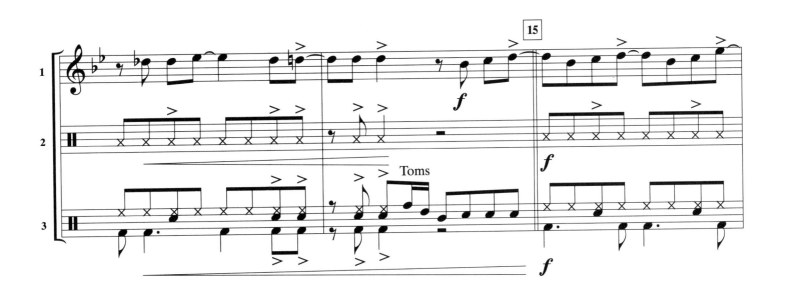

HOW THE WEST WAS WON
Main Title
(From "How the West Was Won" - 1962)

Music by ALFRED NEWMAN
Lyrics by KEN DARBY
Arranged by MICHAEL STORY

IF I ONLY HAD A BRAIN
(From "The Wizard of Oz" - 1939)

Music by HAROLD ARLEN
Lyrics by E.Y. HARBURG
Arranged by MICHAEL STORY

33536

NIMBUS 2000
(From "Harry Potter and the Sorcerer's Stone" - 2001)

By **JOHN WILLIAMS**
Arranged by MICHAEL STORY

Moderately bright

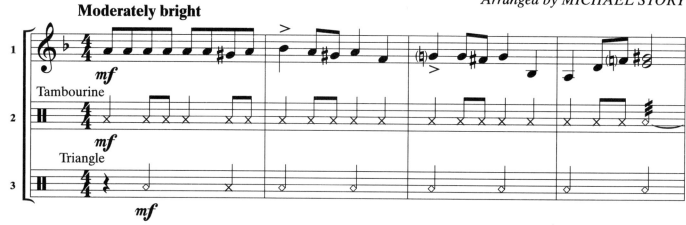

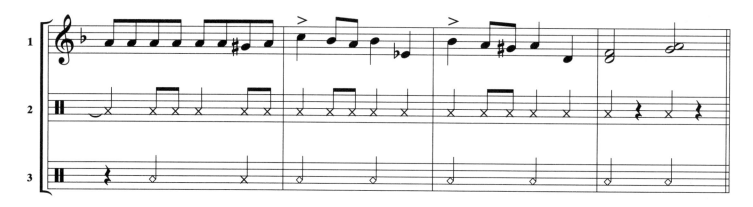

(optional repeat)

YOU'VE GOT A FRIEND IN ME
(From "Toy Story" - 1995)

Words and Music by
RANDY NEWMAN
Arranged by MICHAEL STORY

33536

MAMMA MIA
(From "Mamma Mia!" - 2008)

Words and Music by BENNY ANDERSSON,
STIG ANDERSON and BJORN ULVAEUS
Arranged by MICHAEL STORY

33536

BATMAN THEME
(From "Batman" - 1989)

By DANNY ELFMAN
Arranged by MICHAEL STORY

CANTINA BAND
(From "Star Wars" - 1977)

Music by **JOHN WILLIAMS**
Arranged by MICHAEL STORY

IMPERIAL MARCH
"Darth Vader's Theme"
(From "Star Wars: The Empire Strikes Back" - 1980)

Music by **JOHN WILLIAMS**
Arranged by **MICHAEL STORY**

JAMES BOND THEME
(From the James Bond Series – 1962-2008)

By MONTY NORMAN
Arranged by MICHAEL STORY

THEME FROM "ICE CASTLES"
(Through the Eyes of Love)
(From "Ice Castles" - 1978)

Music by MARVIN HAMLISCH
Lyrics by CAROLE BAYER SAGER
Arranged by MICHAEL STORY

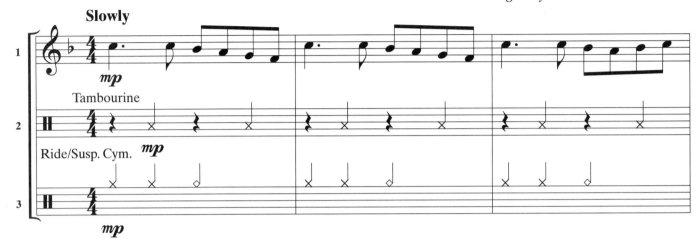

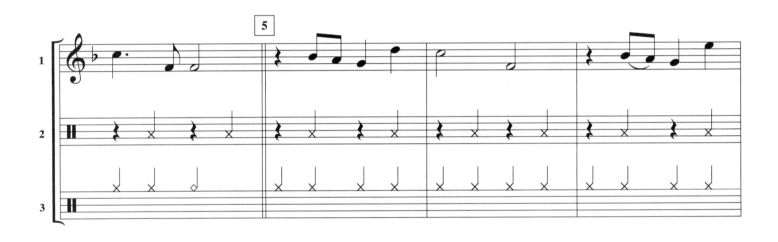

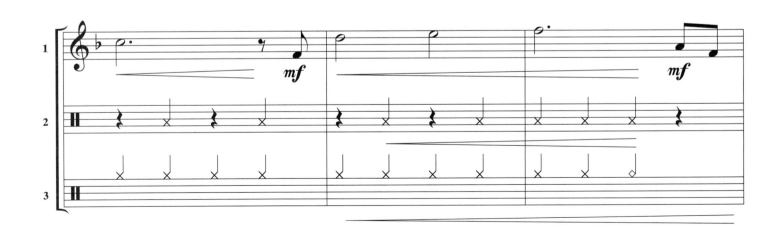

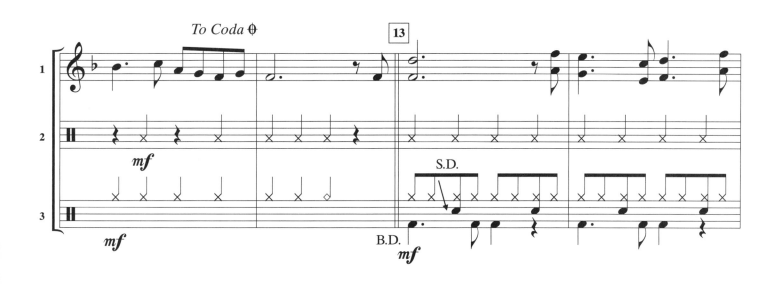

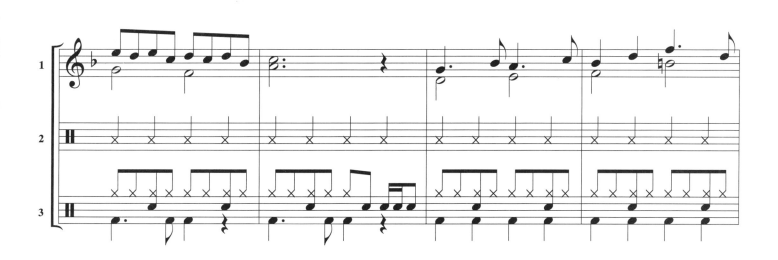

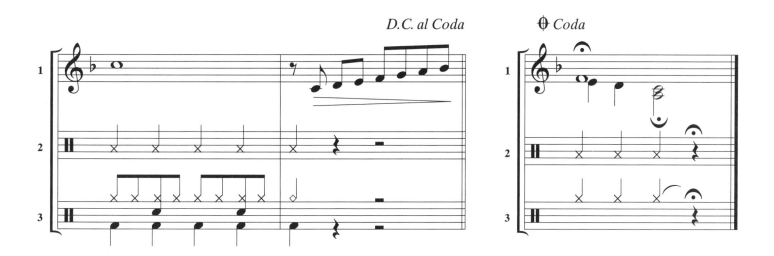

YOU'RE THE ONE THAT I WANT
(From "Grease" - 1978)

Words and Music by
JOHN FARRAR
Arranged by MICHAEL STORY

RAIDERS MARCH
(From "Raiders of the Lost Ark" - 1981)

Music by **JOHN WILLIAMS**
Arranged by MICHAEL STORY